Bring a Torch, Jeannette, Is

Trumpet 2

traditional French carol
arranged by Luther Henderson

Ding Dong! Merrily On High

Trumpet 2

traditional carol
arranged by Luther Henderson

(Play in absence of Chimes-in buckets or into stand.)

Go Tell It On The Mountain

Trumpet 2

19th century Negro Spiritual
arranged by Luther Henderson

God Rest Ye Merry Gentlemen

Flügelhorn 2

traditional London carol, 19th century tune
arranged by Luther Henderson

Here We Come A-Wassailing

Trumpet 2

traditional carol from the north of England
arranged by Luther Henderson

The Huron Carol

Trumpet 2

traditional carol
arranged by Luther Henderson

I Saw Three Ships

Trumpet 2

traditional English carol
arranged by Luther Henderson

Sussex Carol

Trumpet 2

traditional English carol
arranged by Luther Henderson

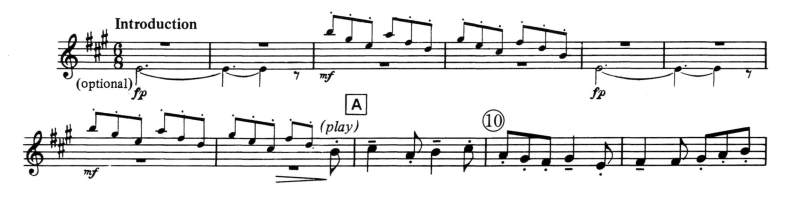

Viola Time Runners

a second book of easy pieces for viola

Kathy and David Blackwell

Illustrations by
Martin Remphry

Welcome to **Viola Time Runners**. You'll find:

- pieces using the finger patterns 0–12–3–4 and 0–1–2–34
- duets, with parts of equal difficulty
- two new pieces, replacing nos. 11 and 16
- a Music Fact-Finder Page at the back to help explain words and signs
- play-along tracks and lively and characterful accompaniments available to download from **www.oup.com/vtrunners2e** or to stream on major streaming platforms
- straightforward piano and viola accompaniments available separately
- a book for viola that's also compatible with Fiddle Time Runners

Teacher's note:

All the pieces in *Viola Time Runners* with the exception of the C string specials can be played together with *Fiddle Time Runners*. There are a few additional pieces in *Fiddle Time Runners* that are not included in the viola book.

 denotes a part that fits with Fiddle Time Runners: these are printed in sequence in the book or on page 30–5. The audio tracks for the pieces listed as 'ensemble parts' are played first by viola and piano, then with the violin part added.

C string special denotes pieces that provide practice on the C string.

OXFORD
UNIVERSITY PRESS

Great Clarendon Street, Oxford OX2 6DP, England
This collection © Oxford University Press 2005 and 2023.
Unless marked otherwise, all pieces are by Kathy and David Blackwell and are
© Oxford University Press. All traditional pieces, and nos. 9, 10, 12, 13, 14, 23, 24, and 30 are
arranged by Kathy and David Blackwell and are © Oxford University Press.
Unauthorized arrangement or photocopying of this copyright material is ILLEGAL.
Kathy and David Blackwell have asserted their right under the Copyright,
Designs and Patents Act, 1988, to be identified as the Composers of this Work.
Impression: 1
ISBN: 978-0-19-356619-4
Music and text origination by Julia Bovee
Printed in Great Britain

Contents